FIRST PEOPLES

COMANCHE

VALERIE BODDEN

CREATIVE EDUCATION ✦ CREATIVE PAPERBACKS

Published by Creative Education and Creative Paperbacks
P.O. Box 227, Mankato, Minnesota 56002
Creative Education and Creative Paperbacks are imprints of
The Creative Company
www.thecreativecompany.us

Design by Christine Vanderbeek
Production by Colin O'Dea
Art direction by Rita Marshall
Printed in the United States of America

Photographs by Alamy (Universal Images Group North
America LLC), Creative Commons Wikimedia (George
A. Addison/Missouri History Museum, George Catlin/
Smithsonian American Art Museum, George Catlin/
Smithsonian American Art Museum/Gift of Mrs. Joseph
Harrison Jr., Fort Sill National Historic Landmark and
Museum, Frontier Forts, Internet Archive Book Images/
Flickr, Sean Pathasema/Birmingham Museum of Art,
Smithsonian Institution/U.S. National Archives and Records
Administration), iStockphoto (Bdphoto, VladSokolovsky),
Shutterstock (Miloje, Emre Tarimcioglu), SuperStock
(Album/Oronoz)

Library of Congress Cataloging-in-Publication Data
Names: Bodden, Valerie, author.
Title: Comanche / Valerie Bodden.
Series: First peoples.
Includes bibliographical references and index.
Summary: An introduction to the Comanche lifestyle and
history, including their forced relocation and how they keep
traditions alive today. A Comanche story recounts how blue-
bonnet flowers came to be.
Identifiers:
ISBN 978-1-64026-224-9 (hardcover)
ISBN 978-1-62832-787-8 (pbk)
ISBN 978-1-64000-359-0 (eBook)
This title has been submitted for CIP processing under LCCN
2019938365.
CCSS: RI.1.1, 2, 3, 4, 5, 6, 7; RI.2.1, 2, 3, 4, 5, 6; RI.3.1, 2, 3, 5;
RF.1.1, 3, 4; RF.2.3, 4

First Edition HC   9 8 7 6 5 4 3 2 1
First Edition PBK   9 8 7 6 5 4 3 2 1

TABLE *of* CONTENTS

SOUTHERN PLAINS PEOPLE

The Comanche lived on the southern GREAT PLAINS. They called themselves *Nermernuh*. This meant "our people." The name *Comanche* probably came from the Ute Indians. It meant "anyone who wants to fight me all the time."

 As the Comanche moved, they often pushed other peoples out of their homelands.

The Comanche lived in small groups for most of the year. These groups were called bands. Each band was led by a head chief.

The men in each Comanche band formed a council, or group that advised the chief.

COMANCHE LIFE

The Comanche lived in tepees. Tepees were made of wooden poles. The poles were covered with bison skins. The Comanche had many horses. They moved often to find new PASTURES for the horses.

 A tepee could be set up in about 15 minutes and taken down in even less time.

Comanche men hunted bison from horseback. They also hunted elk, bears, and deer. The men stole horses. They fought in wars, too.

 The Comanche got horses for hunting animals such as elk by both trading and raiding.

Comanche women gathered wild plants. They cooked meals and made clothing. They worked together to set up and take down tepees. Grandparents helped care for children.

Until about 10 months of age, Comanche babies were strapped into cradleboards to be carried.

COMANCHE CEREMONIES

The Comanche believed spirits were found in nature. Young men went on vision quests. They climbed hills and prayed. They hoped a spirit would give them power.

 Vision quests took seekers away from their camp and family for about four days at a time.

SPANIARDS, SLAVES, AND RESERVATIONS

Spanish SETTLERS already lived on the southern Great Plains when the Comanche arrived. The Comanche stole horses from the settlers. Sometimes they took people to sell as slaves.

 In addition to raiding, the Comanche also traded with Spanish settlers and other tribes.

n the 1870s, the government forced the Comanche off their land. Some fought back. But eventually, they moved to RESERVATIONS. The Comanche were forced to farm instead of hunt. They were not allowed to speak their language.

 Comanche were moved farther south to reservations set up in Texas and Oklahoma.

BEING COMANCHE

Today, many Comanche people still live on the southern Great Plains. Some are learning the Comanche language. They keep their TRADITIONS alive.

Today, Comanche and other Plains tribes join together for traditional dances and ceremonies.

A COMANCHE STORY

The Comanche told stories to explain nature. One story told how it had not rained in a long time. A spirit told the Comanche to SACRIFICE their most important thing to make it rain again. No one wanted to sacrifice anything. But a little girl offered her doll. She burned the doll. Then she spread its ashes. Flowers called bluebonnets grew where the ashes landed. And it rained at last.

GLOSSARY

GREAT PLAINS ✦ grasslands stretching across much of western North America east of the Rocky Mountains

PASTURES ✦ grassy areas where animals can eat

RESERVATIONS ✦ areas of land set aside for American Indians

SACRIFICE ✦ to give up something

SETTLERS ✦ people who come to live in a new area

TRADITIONS ✦ beliefs, stories, or ways of doing things that are passed down from parents to their children

READ MORE

Fullman, Joe. *Native North Americans: Dress, Eat, Write, and Play Just Like the Native Americans*. Mankato, Minn.: QEB, 2010.

Morris, Ting. *Arts and Crafts of the Native Americans*. North Mankato, Minn.: Smart Apple Media, 2007.

WEBSITES

Comanche National Museum and Cultural Center
http://www.comanchemuseum.com/
Learn more about the Comanche way of life.

Texas State Historical Association: Comanche Indians
https://tshaonline.org/handbook/online/articles/bmc72
See paintings and photos of Comanche Indians.

Note: Every effort has been made to ensure that the websites listed above are suitable for children, that they have educational value, and that they contain no inappropriate material. However, because of the nature of the Internet, it is impossible to guarantee that these sites will remain active indefinitely or that their contents will not be altered.

INDEX